The Perfect Package

Homemade treats make wonderful gifts. Whether you're giving muffins, cookies or candy, you'll want to make sure that your present looks as good as it tastes. It's simple—just pack up your goodies in unique containers and decorate them with fun and festive accessories. Use these tips to help create the perfect gift.

- Choose the right basket for what will be going inside: Larger baskets are ideal for muffins, oblong shapes are well suited for breads and smaller baskets are just right for cookies.

- Line baskets with patterned tea towels or attractive napkins. Decorative papers come in a variety of finishes, including glossy and metallic, and these can enhance any gift package. Colorful tissue papers are also perfect for tucking into baskets.

- If you want to wrap up an entire basket filled with treats, use a large roll of cellophane (which can be found at craft and party supply stores). Gather up the ends and secure them with ribbons or cords.

- Ribbons, raffia, satin cords and metallic strings add beautiful finishing touches to any homemade gift. Craft and stationery stores carry a wide variety of these items in every color, size and style imaginable.

- Assorted metal and paper gift tags make excellent personalized cards for your gift basket. You can also personalize plain paper tags with rubber stamps paired with colorful inks—look for stamps with food or holiday themes that will match your gift.

- Before giving your present, remember to include storage directions for perishable items, especially those that must be refrigerated. It's also nice to include serving suggestions with food gifts, or even the recipe itself.

Toffee Crunch Muffins

1½ cups all-purpose flour
⅓ cup packed brown sugar
2 teaspoons baking powder
½ teaspoon baking soda
½ teaspoon salt
½ cup milk
½ cup sour cream
1 egg, beaten
3 tablespoons butter, melted
1 teaspoon vanilla
3 bars (1.4 ounces each) chocolate-covered toffee,
    chopped, divided

1. Preheat oven to 400°F. Grease 36 mini (1¾-inch) muffin cups or line with paper baking cups.

2. Combine flour, sugar, baking powder, baking soda and salt in large bowl. Combine milk, sour cream, egg, butter and vanilla in small bowl until well blended. Stir into flour mixture just until moistened. Fold in two thirds of toffee. Spoon batter into prepared muffin cups, filling almost full. Sprinkle evenly with remaining toffee.

3. Bake 16 to 18 minutes or until toothpick inserted into centers comes out clean. Remove from pans; cool on wire racks 10 minutes. Serve warm or cool completely.

Makes 36 mini muffins

Variation: For regular-size muffins, spoon batter into 10 standard (2½-inch) greased or paper-lined muffin cups. Bake at 350°F about 20 minutes or until toothpick inserted into centers comes out clean.

Pina Colada Cookie Bars

½ cup (1 stick) butter, melted
1½ cups graham cracker crumbs
1 can (14 ounces) sweetened condensed milk
2 tablespoons dark rum
2 cups white chocolate chips
1 cup flaked coconut
½ cup chopped macadamia nuts
½ cup chopped dried pineapple

1. Preheat oven to 350°F.

2. Pour butter into 13×9-inch baking pan, tilting pan to coat bottom evenly with butter. Sprinkle graham cracker crumbs evenly over butter.

3. Blend sweetened condensed milk and rum in small bowl; pour over crumbs. Top with white chips, coconut, nuts and pineapple.

4. Bake 25 to 30 minutes or until edges are lightly browned. Cool in pan on wire rack. Cut into bars with serrated knife. Store loosely covered at room temperature.

Makes 3 dozen bars

Morning Muffins with Blueberries

½ cup plus 1 tablespoon sugar, divided
⅛ teaspoon ground cinnamon
1¾ cups all-purpose flour
2 teaspoons baking powder
½ teaspoon salt
½ cup milk
¼ cup vegetable oil
1 egg
1 teaspoon vanilla
1 teaspoon grated orange peel
1 cup fresh or frozen blueberries, thawed and dried

1. Preheat oven to 400°F. Grease 12 standard (2½-inch) muffin cups or line with paper baking cups. Combine 1 tablespoon sugar and cinnamon in small bowl; set aside.

2. Combine flour, remaining ½ cup sugar, baking powder and salt in large bowl. Beat milk, oil, egg, vanilla and orange peel in small bowl until blended. Make a well in center of flour mixture; stir in milk mixture just until moistened. Fold in blueberries. Spoon evenly into prepared muffin cups, filling about two-thirds full.

3. Bake 15 to 18 minutes or until toothpick inserted into centers comes out clean. Immediately sprinkle sugar mixture over hot muffins. Remove from pan; cool on wire rack. Serve warm or at room temperature. *Makes 12 muffins*

Tip: For muffins with larger tops, fill the prepared muffin cups almost full and bake at 400°F about 20 minutes or until a toothpick inserted into the centers comes out clean. Proceed as directed above. (The recipe will make about 8 big-top muffins.)

Breadstick Sampler

1 package (11 ounces) refrigerated breadstick dough (8 breadsticks)
1 tablespoon grated Parmesan cheese
¹⁄₈ teaspoon ground red pepper
¹⁄₂ teaspoon dried basil
¹⁄₂ teaspoon dried oregano
¹⁄₂ teaspoon dried thyme
2 tablespoons olive oil
1 tablespoon garlic powder, divided

1. Preheat oven to 350°F. Grease baking sheet. Separate and unroll strips of dough. Twist each breadstick several times and place about 1 inch apart on prepared baking sheet. Press ends firmly onto baking sheet.

2. Combine Parmesan and red pepper in small bowl. Combine basil, oregano and thyme in another small bowl.

3. Brush all breadsticks with olive oil. Sprinkle 2 breadsticks with 1 teaspoon garlic powder each. Sprinkle 2 breaksticks with 1 teaspoon Parmesan mixture each. Sprinkle 2 breadsticks with ¹⁄₂ teaspoon herb mixture each. For remaining 2 breadsticks, sprinkle each with remaining garlic powder, cheese mixture and herb mixture.

4. Bake 15 minutes or until golden brown. Remove from baking sheet; cool on wire rack 5 minutes. Serve warm.

Makes 8 breadsticks

Note: You can vary this recipe by sprinkling the breadsticks with your own favorite toppings. Try sesame or poppy seeds, seasoned salt, onion powder or cinnamon and sugar.

Double Chocolate Zucchini Muffins

2 1/3 cups all-purpose flour
1 1/4 cups sugar
  1/3 cup unsweetened cocoa powder
  2 teaspoons baking powder
1 1/2 teaspoons ground cinnamon
  1 teaspoon baking soda
  1/2 teaspoon salt
  1 cup sour cream
  1/2 cup vegetable oil
  2 eggs, beaten
  1/4 cup milk
  1 cup milk chocolate chips
  1 cup shredded zucchini

1. Preheat oven to 400°F. Grease 12 jumbo (3 1/2-inch) muffin cups or line with paper baking cups.

2. Combine flour, sugar, cocoa, baking powder, cinnamon, baking soda and salt in large bowl. Combine sour cream, oil, eggs and milk in small bowl until blended; stir into flour mixture just until moistened. Fold in chocolate chips and zucchini. Spoon into prepared muffin cups, filling about half full.

3. Bake 25 to 30 minutes until toothpick inserted into centers comes out clean. Cool in pan 5 minutes; remove from pan and cool completely on wire rack. Store tightly covered at room temperature. *Makes 12 jumbo muffins*

Variation: For regular-size muffins, spoon batter into 18 standard (2 1/2-inch) greased or paper-lined muffin cups. Bake at 400°F 18 to 20 minutes or until toothpick inserted into centers comes out clean.

Irish Soda Bread Rounds

4 cups all-purpose flour
¼ cup sugar
1 tablespoon baking powder
1 teaspoon baking soda
1 teaspoon salt
⅓ cup shortening
1 cup currants or raisins
1¾ cups buttermilk
1 egg

1. Preheat oven to 350°F. Grease two baking sheets.

2. Sift flour, sugar, baking powder, baking soda and salt into large bowl. Cut in shortening with pastry blender or two knives until mixture resembles coarse crumbs. Stir in currants. Beat buttermilk and egg in medium bowl until well blended. Add buttermilk mixture to flour mixture; stir until mixture forms soft dough that clings together and forms a ball.

3. Turn out dough onto well-floured surface. Knead dough gently 10 to 12 times. Shape dough into 8 (3½-inch) rounds; place rounds on prepared baking sheets. Score top of each round with tip of sharp knife, making an "X" about 1 inch long and ¼ inch deep.

4. Bake 25 to 28 minutes or until toothpick inserted into centers comes out clean. Immediately remove breads from baking sheets; cool on wire racks.*   *Makes 8 rounds*

For a sweet crust, combine 1 tablespoon sugar and 1 tablespoon water in small bowl; brush over hot bread.

14

15

Raspberry Pecan Thumbprints

2 cups all-purpose flour
1 cup pecan pieces, finely chopped, divided
½ teaspoon ground cinnamon
¼ teaspoon ground allspice
⅛ teaspoon salt
1 cup (2 sticks) butter, softened
½ cup packed light brown sugar
2 teaspoons vanilla
⅓ cup seedless raspberry jam

1. Preheat oven to 350°F. Combine flour, ½ cup pecans, cinnamon, allspice and salt in medium bowl.

2. Beat butter in large bowl with electric mixer at medium speed until smooth. Gradually beat in brown sugar; beat until light and fluffy. Beat in vanilla until blended. Beat in flour mixture just until blended.

3. Shape dough into 1-inch balls; flatten slightly and place on ungreased cookie sheets. Press down with thumb in center of each ball to form indentation. Pinch together any cracks in dough. Fill each indentation with generous ¼ teaspoon jam. Sprinkle filled cookies with remaining ½ cup pecans.

4. Bake 14 minutes or until just set. Cool on cookie sheets 5 minutes; remove to wire racks to cool completely. Store in airtight container at room temperature. Cookies are best the day after baking.   *Makes 3 dozen cookies*

Bacon Cheddar Muffins

2 cups all-purpose flour
¾ cup sugar
2 teaspoons baking powder
½ teaspoon baking soda
½ teaspoon salt
¾ cup plus 2 tablespoons milk
⅓ cup butter, melted
1 egg, lightly beaten
1 cup (4 ounces) shredded Cheddar cheese
½ cup crumbled crisp-cooked bacon (about 6 slices)

1. Preheat oven to 350°F. Grease 12 standard (2½-inch) muffin cups or line with paper baking cups.

2. Combine flour, sugar, baking powder, baking soda and salt in medium bowl. Combine milk, butter and egg in small bowl; mix well. Add milk mixture to flour mixture; stir just until blended. Gently stir in cheese and bacon. Spoon evenly into prepared muffin cups, filling three-quarters full.

3. Bake 15 to 20 minutes or until toothpick inserted into centers comes out clean. Cool in pan 2 minutes; remove to wire rack. Serve warm or at room temperature. *Makes 12 muffins*

Peanut Butter Jumbos

1½ cups peanut butter
1 cup granulated sugar
1 cup packed brown sugar
3 eggs
½ cup (1 stick) butter, softened
1 teaspoon vanilla
4½ cups uncooked old-fashioned oats
2 teaspoons baking soda
1 cup (6 ounces) semisweet chocolate chips
1 cup candy-coated chocolate pieces

1. Preheat oven to 350°F. Lightly grease cookie sheets or line with parchment paper.

2. Beat peanut butter, granulated sugar, brown sugar, eggs, butter and vanilla in large bowl until well blended. Stir in oats and baking soda until well blended. Stir in chocolate chips and candy pieces.

3. Scoop out about ⅓ cup dough for each cookie. Place on prepared cookie sheets, spacing about 4 inches apart. Press each cookie to flatten slightly. Bake 15 to 20 minutes or until firm in center. Remove to wire racks to cool.

Makes about 1½ dozen cookies

Apple Butter Spice Muffins

½ cup sugar
1 teaspoon ground cinnamon
¼ teaspoon ground nutmeg
⅛ teaspoon ground allspice
½ cup pecans or walnuts, chopped
2 cups all-purpose flour
2 teaspoons baking powder
¼ teaspoon salt
1 cup milk
¼ cup vegetable oil
1 egg
¼ cup apple butter

1. Preheat oven to 400°F. Grease 12 standard (2½-inch) muffin cups or line with paper baking cups.

2. Combine sugar, cinnamon, nutmeg and allspice in large bowl. Toss 2 tablespoons sugar mixture with pecans in small bowl. Add flour, baking powder and salt to remaining sugar mixture. Combine milk, oil and egg in medium bowl. Stir into flour mixture just until moistened.

3. Spoon 1 tablespoon batter into each muffin cup. Spoon 1 teaspoon apple butter into each cup; top with remaining batter. Sprinkle with reserved pecan mixture.

4. Bake 20 to 25 minutes or until golden brown and toothpick inserted into centers comes out clean. Immediately remove from pan; cool on wire rack 10 minutes. Serve warm or cool completely.

Makes 12 muffins

Tomato-Artichoke Focaccia

1 package (16 ounces) hot roll mix
2 tablespoons wheat bran
1¼ cups hot water
4 teaspoons olive oil, divided
1 cup thinly sliced onions
2 cloves garlic, minced
4 ounces sun-dried tomatoes (not packed in oil),
  rehydrated* and cut into strips
1 cup canned artichoke hearts, cut into quarters
1 tablespoon minced fresh rosemary
2 tablespoons shredded Parmesan cheese

To rehydrate sun-dried tomatoes, pour 1 cup boiling water over tomatoes in small heatproof bowl. Let tomatoes soak 5 to 10 minutes until softened; drain well.

1. Preheat oven to 400°F. Combine dry ingredients and yeast packet from hot roll mix in large bowl. Add bran; mix well. Stir in hot water and 2 teaspoons oil. Knead dough about 5 minutes or until ingredients are blended.

2. Spray two 9-inch round cake pans with nonstick cooking spray. Press dough onto bottom of prepared pans. Cover and let rise 15 minutes.

3. Heat 1 teaspoon oil in medium skillet over low heat. Add onions and garlic; cook and stir 2 to 3 minutes until onions are tender. Brush surface of dough with remaining 1 teaspoon oil. Top dough with onion mixture, tomatoes, artichokes and rosemary. Sprinkle with Parmesan.

4. Bake 25 to 30 minutes or until lightly browned. Remove from pans; cool on wire racks.   *Makes 16 servings*

Chewy Peanut Butter Brownies

¾ **cup (1½ sticks) butter, melted**
¾ **cup creamy peanut butter**
1¾ **cups sugar**
  2 **teaspoons vanilla**
  4 **eggs, lightly beaten**
1¼ **cups all-purpose flour**
  ½ **teaspoon baking powder**
  ¼ **teaspoon salt**
  ¼ **cup unsweetened cocoa powder**

1. Preheat oven to 350°F. Grease 13×9-inch baking pan.

2. Combine butter and peanut butter in large bowl; mix well. Stir in sugar and vanilla. Add eggs; beat until well blended. Stir in flour, baking powder and salt just until blended. Remove 1¾ cups batter to small bowl; stir cocoa into reserved batter.

3. Spread cocoa batter evenly in bottom of prepared pan. Top with remaining batter. Bake 30 minutes or until edges begin to pull away from sides of pan. Cool completely in pan on wire rack. Cut into bars. *Makes about 2 dozen brownies*

27

Chocolate Chip Shortbread

½ cup (1 stick) butter, softened
½ cup sugar
1 teaspoon vanilla
1 cup all-purpose flour
¼ teaspoon salt
½ cup mini semisweet chocolate chips

1. Preheat oven to 375°F.

2. Beat butter and sugar in large bowl with electric mixer at medium speed until light and fluffy. Beat in vanilla. Add flour and salt; beat at low speed. Stir in chocolate chips.

3. Divide dough in half. Press each half into ungreased 8-inch round cake pan.

4. Bake 12 minutes or until edges are golden brown. Score shortbread with sharp knife (8 triangles per pan), taking care not to cut completely through shortbread.

5. Cool in pans on wire racks 10 minutes. Invert shortbread onto wire racks and cool completely. Break into triangles.

Makes 16 cookies

Streusel-Topped Raspberry Muffins

2¼ cups all-purpose flour, divided
¼ cup packed brown sugar
2 tablespoons butter
¾ cup granulated sugar
2 teaspoons baking powder
½ teaspoon baking soda
½ teaspoon salt
½ teaspoon grated lemon peel
¾ cup plus 2 tablespoons milk
⅓ cup butter, melted
1 egg, beaten
2 cups fresh or frozen raspberries (do not thaw)

1. Preheat oven to 350°F. Grease 6 jumbo (3½-inch) muffin cups. For topping, combine ¼ cup flour and brown sugar in small bowl. Cut in 2 tablespoons butter with pastry blender or two knives until mixture forms coarse clumps.

2. Reserve ¼ cup flour; set aside. Combine remaining 1¾ cups flour, granulated sugar, baking powder, baking soda, salt and lemon peel in medium bowl. Combine milk, melted butter and egg in small bowl.

3. Add milk mixture to flour mixture; stir until almost blended. Toss raspberries with reserved flour in medium bowl just until coated; gently fold raspberries into muffin batter. Spoon batter into prepared muffin cups, filling three-quarters full. Sprinkle with topping.

4. Bake 25 to 30 minutes or until toothpick inserted into centers comes out clean. Cool in pan 2 minutes; remove to wire rack. Serve warm or at room temperature.

Makes 6 jumbo muffins

Tiger Stripes

1 package (12 ounces) semisweet chocolate chips
3 tablespoons creamy or chunky peanut butter, divided
2 (2-ounce) white chocolate baking bars

1. Line 8-inch square pan with foil; lightly grease foil.

2. Melt semisweet chocolate and 2 tablespoons peanut butter in small saucepan over low heat; stir until melted and smooth. Pour chocolate mixture into prepared pan. Let stand 10 to 15 minutes to cool slightly.

3. Melt white chocolate and remaining 1 tablespoon peanut butter in small saucepan over low heat; stir until melted and smooth. Drop spoonfuls of white chocolate mixture over semisweet chocolate mixture in pan. Using small metal spatula or knife, swirl chocolates to create tiger stripes.

4. Freeze about 1 hour or until firm. Remove from pan; peel off foil. Cut or break into pieces. Refrigerate until ready to serve.

Makes 3 dozen pieces

Brunchtime Sour Cream Cupcakes

  2 cups plus 4 teaspoons sugar, divided
  1 cup (2 sticks) butter, softened
  2 eggs
  1 cup sour cream
  1 teaspoon almond extract
  2 cups all-purpose flour
  1 teaspoon salt
  ½ teaspoon baking soda
  1 cup chopped walnuts
1½ teaspoons ground cinnamon
  ⅛ teaspoon ground nutmeg

1. Preheat oven to 350°F. Lightly grease 18 standard (2½-inch) muffin cups or line with paper baking cups.

2. Beat 2 cups sugar and butter in large bowl. Add eggs, one at a time, beating well after each addition. Blend in sour cream and almond extract. Combine flour, salt and baking soda in medium bowl. Add to butter mixture; mix well. Combine remaining 4 teaspoons sugar, walnuts, cinnamon and nutmeg in small bowl.

3. Fill prepared muffin cups one-third full with batter; sprinkle evenly with two-thirds of walnut mixture. Top with remaining batter; sprinkle with remaining walnut mixture.

4. Bake 25 to 30 minutes or until toothpick inserted into centers comes out clean. Remove from pans; cool on wire racks.

Makes 18 cupcakes

Pumpkin Oatmeal Cookies

    1 cup all-purpose flour
    1 teaspoon cinnamon
  $\frac{1}{2}$ teaspoon salt
  $\frac{1}{2}$ teaspoon ground nutmeg
  $\frac{1}{4}$ teaspoon baking soda
 1$\frac{1}{2}$ cups firmly packed light brown sugar
  $\frac{1}{2}$ cup (1 stick) butter, softened
    1 egg
    1 teaspoon vanilla
  $\frac{1}{2}$ cup canned pumpkin
    2 cups uncooked old-fashioned oats
    1 cup dried cranberries (optional)

1. Preheat oven to 350°F. Line cookie sheets with parchment paper.

2. Sift flour, cinnamon, salt, nutmeg and baking soda into medium bowl. Beat brown sugar and butter in large bowl with electric mixer at medium speed about 5 minutes or until light and fluffy. Beat in egg and vanilla. Add pumpkin; beat at low speed until blended. Beat in flour mixture just until blended. Add oats; mix well. Stir in cranberries, if desired.

3. Drop batter by generous tablespoonfuls about 2 inches apart on prepared cookie sheets.

4. Bake 12 minutes or until golden brown. Cool on cookie sheets 1 minute; remove to wire racks to cool completely.

Makes about 2 dozen cookies

Mocha-Macadamia Nut Muffins

1¼ cups all-purpose flour
⅔ cup granulated sugar
2½ tablespoons unsweetened cocoa powder
1 teaspoon baking soda
¼ teaspoon salt
⅔ cup buttermilk*
1 egg, beaten
3 tablespoons butter, melted
1 tablespoon instant coffee granules dissolved in
  1 tablespoon hot water
¾ teaspoon vanilla
½ cup coarsely chopped macadamia nuts
Powdered sugar (optional)

*Soured fresh milk can be substituted for buttermilk. To sour milk, combine 2 teaspoons lemon juice plus enough milk to equal ⅔ cup. Stir; let stand 5 minutes before using.

1. Preheat oven to 400°F. Lightly grease 12 standard (2½-inch) muffin cups or line with paper baking cups.

2. Combine flour, granulated sugar, cocoa, baking soda and salt in large bowl. Combine buttermilk, egg, butter, coffee mixture and vanilla in medium bowl; beat until blended. Stir buttermilk mixture into flour mixture just until dry ingredients are moistened. Stir in macadamia nuts. Spoon batter evenly into prepared muffin cups.

3. Bake 13 to 17 minutes or until toothpick inserted into centers comes out clean. Cool in pan on wire rack 5 minutes; remove from pan and cool 10 minutes on wire rack. Sprinkle with powdered sugar, if desired.   *Makes 12 muffins*

Snickerdoodles

¾ cup sugar plus 1 tablespoon sugar, divided
2 teaspoons cinnamon, divided
1⅓ cups all-purpose flour
1 teaspoon cream of tartar
½ teaspoon baking soda
½ cup (1 stick) butter
1 egg
1 package (6 ounces) cinnamon baking chips
1 cup raisins (optional)

1. Preheat oven to 400°F. Combine 1 tablespoon sugar and 1 teaspoon cinnamon in small bowl; set aside.

2. Combine flour, remaining 1 teaspoon cinnamon, cream of tartar and baking soda in medium bowl. Beat remaining ¾ cup sugar and butter in large bowl with electric mixer at medium speed until creamy. Beat in egg. Gradually add flour mixture to sugar mixture, beating at low speed until stiff dough forms. Stir in cinnamon chips and raisins, if desired.

3. Roll tablespoonfuls of dough into 1-inch balls; roll balls in sugar mixture. Place on ungreased cookie sheets.

4. Bake 10 minutes or until firm in center. *Do not overbake.* Remove from cookie sheets; cool completely on wire racks.

Makes about 3 dozen cookies

Tex-Mex Quick Bread

1½ cups all-purpose flour
1 cup (4 ounces) shredded Monterey Jack cheese
½ cup cornmeal
½ cup coarsely chopped sun-dried tomatoes packed in oil
1 can (about 4 ounces) black olives, drained and chopped
¼ cup sugar
1½ teaspoons baking powder
1 teaspoon baking soda
1 cup milk
1 can (about 4 ounces) green chiles, drained and chopped
¼ cup olive oil
1 egg, beaten

1. Preheat oven to 325°F. Grease 9×5-inch loaf pan or four small (5×3-inch) loaf pans.

2. Combine flour, cheese, cornmeal, tomatoes, olives, sugar, baking powder and baking soda in large bowl. Combine milk, chiles, oil and egg in small bowl. Stir milk mixture into flour mixture just until dry ingredients are moistened. Pour into prepared pan.

3. Bake large loaf 45 minutes and small loaves 30 minutes or until toothpick inserted into center comes out clean. Cool in pan on wire rack 15 minutes; remove from pan and cool completely on wire rack.   *Makes 1 large loaf or 4 small loaves*

Muffin Variation: Preheat oven to 375°F. Spoon batter into 12 well-greased muffin cups. Bake 20 minutes or until toothpick inserted into centers comes out clean. Makes 12 muffins.

Mississippi Mud Bars

¾ **cup packed brown sugar**
½ **cup butter, softened**
1 **egg**
1 **teaspoon vanilla**
½ **teaspoon baking soda**
¼ **teaspoon salt**
1 **cup plus 2 tablespoons all-purpose flour**
1 **cup (6 ounces) semisweet chocolate chips, divided**
1 **cup (6 ounces) white chocolate chips, divided**
½ **cup chopped walnuts or pecans**

1. Preheat oven to 375°F. Line 9-inch square pan with foil; grease foil.

2. Beat sugar and butter in large bowl until well blended. Beat in egg and vanilla until light. Blend in baking soda and salt. Add flour, mixing until well blended. Stir in ⅔ cup semisweet chips, ⅔ cup white chips and nuts. Spread dough in prepared pan.

3. Bake 23 to 25 minutes or until center feels firm. Remove from oven; sprinkle with remaining ⅓ cup semisweet chips and ⅓ cup white chips. Let stand until chips melt; spread evenly over bars. Cool in pan on wire rack until chocolate is set. Cut into bars or triangles.   *Makes about 3 dozen bars*

Cranberry Brunch Muffins

1 cup chopped fresh cranberries
1/3 cup plus 1/4 cup sugar, divided
2 cups all-purpose flour
2 teaspoons baking powder
3/4 teaspoon salt
1/2 cup (1 stick) butter
3/4 cup orange juice
1 egg, lightly beaten
1 teaspoon vanilla
2 tablespoons butter, melted

1. Preheat oven to 400°F. Lightly grease 12 standard (2½-inch) muffin cups or line with paper baking cups.

2. Combine cranberries and 1 tablespoon sugar in small bowl. Combine flour, 1/3 cup sugar, baking powder and salt in large bowl. Cut in 1/2 cup butter with pastry blender or two knives until mixture is crumbly. Stir in orange juice, egg and vanilla just until ingredients are moistened. Fold in cranberry mixture; spoon batter evenly into prepared muffin cups.

3. Bake 20 to 25 minutes or until golden brown. Cool in pan 5 minutes. Remove from pan; dip tops of muffins in melted butter and sprinkle with remaining 3 tablespoons sugar.

Makes 12 muffins